Married Life Be Like

COLORING TEST PAGE

COLORING TEST PAGE

In our MARRIAGE everything is 50/50.
I COOK, he **eats**.
I WASH, he **wears**.
I SHOP, he **pays**!

A happy marriage is a long conversation which always seems too short.

The secret to a
happy marriage
remains a
SECRET.

When **TWO PEOPLE** love each
other, they **do not** look at each
other, they look in the *same direction*,
and that path is *Marriage*.

Bonus!

Some remain **single** and make *wonders*' happen.
Some have **boyfriends** and see *wonders* happen.
The rest get MARRIED and wonder **what happened**.

A happy marriage is a long conversation which always seems too short.

The secret to a
happy marriage
remains a
SECRET.

A happy marriage is the union of two good forgivers.

When **TWO PEOPLE** love each other, they **do not** look at each other, they look in the *same direction*, and that path is *Marriage*.

Made in the USA
Las Vegas, NV
29 November 2021